PRAYING
THE PSALMS

JUANITA
RYAN

9 STUDIES
FOR INDIVIDUALS
OR GROUPS

Life
Builder
Study

INTER-VARSITY PRESS
36 Causton Street, London SW1P 4ST, England
Email: ivp@ivpbooks.com
Website: www.ivpbooks.com

© Juanita Ryan, 1995, 2003
First UK edition © Scripture Union, 2003
This edition © Inter-Varsity Press, 2019

Juanita Ryan has asserted her right under the Copyright, Designs and Patents Act 1988
to be identified as Author of this work.

All rights reserved. No part of this publication may be reproduced, stored in a retrieval
system, or transmitted, in any form or by any means, electronic, mechanical,
photocopying, recording or otherwise, without the prior permission of the publisher
or the Copyright Licensing Agency.

Scripture quotations are taken from The Holy Bible, New International Version. Copyright
© 1973, 1978, 1984 by International Bible Society. Anglicization copyright © 1979,
1984, 1989. Used by permission of Hodder & Stoughton Publishers, a member of the
Hachette UK Group. All rights reserved. 'NIV' is a registered trademark of International
Bible Society. UK trademark number 1448790.

*Originally published in the United States of America in the LifeGuide® Bible Studies series
in 1995 by InterVarsity Press, Downers Grove, Illinois*
Second edition published 2003
First published in Great Britain by Scripture Union in 2003
This edition published in Great Britain by Inter-Varsity Press 2019

British Library Cataloguing-in-Publication Data
A catalogue record for this book is available from the British Library.

ISBN: 978–1–78359–827–4

Printed in Great Britain by Ashford Colour Press Ltd, Gosport, Hampshire

*Inter-Varsity Press publishes Christian books that are true to the Bible and that communicate
the gospel, develop discipleship and strengthen the church for its mission in the world.*

*IVP originated within the Inter-Varsity Fellowship, now the Universities and Colleges Christian
Fellowship, a student movement connecting Christian Unions in universities and colleges
throughout Great Britain, and a member movement of the International Fellowship of
Evangelical Students. Website: www.uccf.org.uk. That historic association is maintained,
and all senior IVP staff and committee members subscribe to the UCCF Basis of Faith.*

Contents

GETTING THE MOST OUT OF *PRAYING THE PSALMS* —————— 5

1 A Prayer of Dependence   Psalm 86 ————— 9

2 A Prayer of Longing for God   Psalm 63 ————— 13

3 A Prayer of Trust   Psalm 62 ————— 17

4 A Prayer of Distress   Psalm 57 ————— 21

5 A Prayer of Gratitude   Psalm 65 ————— 25

6 A Prayer of Grief   Psalm 102 ————— 29

7 A Prayer When God Is Silent   Psalm 44 ————— 34

8 A Prayer for Hope   Psalm 130 ————— 39

9 A Prayer of Joy   Psalm 66 ————— 44

LEADER'S NOTES ————————————— 48

Getting the Most Out of
Praying the Psalms

The psalms are acts of relating to God. In the intense language of poetry, they address God with frankness and urgency. They give voice to our inner turmoil. They teach us to talk to God about life's deepest needs and longings with childlike vulnerability and spontaneity. They immerse us in a spiritual life that is a passionate struggle to love and to know we are loved by God.

The psalms offer us the gifts of expression, courage and celebration—and the gift of raw honesty. The psalms do not attempt to be "nice" or "polite" or even "theologically correct." Instead, they give us permission to talk to God without holding back and to be exactly where we are and who we are with God.

The psalms offer us the gift of expression. They give us powerful words and images which express our heart cry to God. The private realities that we hesitate to speak out loud to ourselves or to God are given voice. Our fears, our hopes, our joy, our anger, our longing, our gratitude, our doubt and our worship find full expression here.

In addition, the psalms give us the gift of courage, particularly the courage to acknowledge our vulnerable dependence on God. We greatly prefer to think of ourselves as invulnerable and independent. It takes courage to admit the truth of our dependency on God. But, like all truth, this truth frees us. It frees us to be who we are. It frees us to let God be God, and to let ourselves be his children.

Finally, the psalms give us the gift of celebration. They call us to shout, sing and dance our gratitude and praise to God. The psalms draw us into active worship. They take us by the hand and lead us to a grand party where the gifts of life and love are celebrated and God is praised. As we enter the world of the psalms, we come into God's presence as the vulnerable, honest, needy, spontaneous, joyful children he made us to be.

May you find the gifts of honesty, expression, courage and celebration the psalms offer you. May they bring new depth and vitality to your relationship with God.

Suggestions for Individual Study

1. As you begin each study, pray that God will speak to you through his Word.

2. Read the introduction to the study and respond to the personal reflection question or exercise. This is designed to help you focus on God and on the theme of the study.

3. Each study deals with a particular passage—so that you can delve into the author's meaning in that context. Read and reread the passage to be studied. The questions are written using the language of the New International Version, so you may wish to use that version of the Bible. The New Revised Standard Version is also recommended.

4. This is an inductive Bible study, designed to help you discover for yourself what Scripture is saying. The study includes three types of questions. *Observation* questions ask about the basic facts: who, what, when, where and how. *Interpretation* questions delve into the meaning of the passage. *Application* questions help you discover the implications of the text for growing in Christ. These three keys unlock the treasures of Scripture.

Write your answers to the questions in the spaces provided or in a personal journal. Writing can bring clarity and deeper understanding of yourself and of God's Word.

5. It might be good to have a Bible dictionary handy. Use it to look up any unfamiliar words, names or places.

6. Use the prayer suggestion to guide you in thanking God for what you have learned and to pray about the applications that have come to mind.

7. You may want to go on to the suggestion under "Now or Later," or you may want to use that idea for your next study.

Suggestions for Members of a Group Study

1. Come to the study prepared. Follow the suggestions for individual study mentioned above. You will find that careful preparation will greatly enrich your time spent in group discussion.

2. Be willing to participate in the discussion. The leader of your group will not be lecturing. Instead, he or she will be encouraging the members of the group to discuss what they have learned. The leader will be asking the questions that are found in this guide.

3. Stick to the topic being discussed. Your answers should be based on the verses which are the focus of the discussion and not on outside authorities such as commentaries or speakers. These studies focus on a particular passage of Scripture. Only rarely should you refer to other portions of the Bible. This allows for everyone to participate in in-depth study on equal ground.

4. Be sensitive to the other members of the group. Listen attentively when they describe what they have learned. You may be surprised by their insights! Each question assumes a variety of answers. Many questions do not have "right" answers, particularly questions that aim at meaning or application. Instead the questions push us to explore the passage more thoroughly.

When possible, link what you say to the comments of others. Also, be affirming whenever you can. This will encourage some of the more hesitant members of the group to participate. **5.** Be careful not to dominate the discussion. We are sometimes so eager to express our thoughts that we leave too little opportunity for others to respond. By all means participate! But allow others to also.

6. Expect God to teach you through the passage being discussed and through the other members of the group. Pray that you will have an enjoyable and profitable time together, but also that as a result of the study you will find ways that you can take action individually and/or as a group.

7. Remember that anything said in the group is considered confidential and should not be discussed outside the group unless specific permission is given to do so.

8. If you are the group leader, you will find additional suggestions at the back of the guide.

1

A Prayer of Dependence

Psalm 86

Our relationship with God is that of children to a parent, sheep to a shepherd, creatures to the Creator. We are dependent on him for life, for breath, for sustenance, for help in trouble, for love, for forgiveness, for mercy. We may like to think of ourselves as independent and self-sufficient, but we are not. We need God. It is vital that we acknowledge our need because it is the beginning point of our relationship with him.

GROUP DISCUSSION. Take a few minutes to write about a young child and a loving parent you have known or know currently. What kind of help does the child need from his parent? What is it like to watch a child depending on her parent? Read what you have written to one another.

PERSONAL REFLECTION. Think of a time when you needed to rely on someone for emotional or physical support. What feelings did you have about depending on that person for help?

This psalm helps us give voice to our dependence on God. *Read Psalm 86.*

1. What is the overall sense you get about the nature of the psalmist's relationship with God?

2. What appeals to you about the psalmist's relationship with God?

3. List the many requests the psalmist makes of God.

4. The psalmist describes himself in the first verse as "poor and needy." What is he saying about himself?

5. What reactions would you have to describing yourself as poor and needy?

---

6. Why does the psalmist need God's help?

---

7. What are some of the specific statements the psalmist makes about God?

---

8. How would you summarize the psalmist's view of God?

---

9. How does the psalmist show his dependence on God throughout this psalm?

10. When is it difficult for you to depend on God?

11. How might the psalmist's dependency on God encourage you to depend more fully on God?

12. In what areas of your life do you need to acknowledge your dependence on God?

Spend some time acknowledging in prayer some of the specific ways you need God at this time in your life.

Now or Later

Write about a time when you experienced God's help and presence. Write a prayer, thanking God for this memory and expressing your need for God today.

2

A Prayer of Longing for God

Sometimes we feel separated from God. During these times, we may feel much like small children feel when they are separated from their parents—frightened, angry. And we may experience an intense longing for our parent to return.

Many things can create this sense of separation from God. It might come as a result of a loss or crisis in our lives which leaves us feeling forgotten or uncared for by God. It might come during a time of personal sin or failure when we struggle with fear that God might condemn or reject us. It might come as a result of being removed from our community of faith. Whatever the reason, a sense of separation from God can generate an intense longing for God

GROUP DISCUSSION. Have two people in the group do a series of "living sculptures." Have them stand in the center of the group with their backs to each other and their arms folded across their chests. Then have one of them turn to face the other's back with arms reaching out. And finally, have the two of them face each other with arms reaching out to each other. Afterward, have group members briefly write what it might feel like to be each person in each sculpture. Take some time to discuss what people have written about feelings regarding the experience of separation and the experience of reconnection.

PERSONAL REFLECTION. Think of a time when you felt especially close to God. What was the experience like for you?

This psalm helps us express our longing for God in times when we feel separated from him. *Read Psalm 63.*

1. How does David's present experience of God differ from his past experience (vv. 1-2)?

2. The psalmist describes his experience of longing for God in verse 1 with the strong physical metaphor of being thirsty in a desert with no sign of water. How is this image an appropriate description of what it feels like to be separated from God?

3. In verses 2 and 3 the psalmist describes how, in the past, he experienced God's presence. What did he experience of God?

4. Verse 1 describes a soul that is thirsty, with no chance of

finding water. In stark contrast, verse 5 describes a soul that is satisfied with the richest of foods. These pictures contrast the experience of being separated from God and the experience of being close to God. What words or images would you use to describe times when you have felt separated from God?

---

5. What words or images would you use to describe times when you felt close to God?

---

6. Because of his longing for connection with God, the psalmist says he will seek God, he will remember God, and he will cling to God. The first action he takes is to earnestly seek God (v. 1). What does it mean to seek God?

---

7. The second action he takes is "remembering." Where, when, how and in what way does the psalmist say he "remembers" God (vv. 6-7)?

---

8. What value is there in remembering past experiences of God when we feel separated from him?

9. The third action he describes is "clinging." In verse 8 he describes how he clings to God and how God holds him. What is your response to the image of clinging to God?

———————————————————————————————

10. In the final phrases the psalmist responds in joy to the hope of once again experiencing God's presence. How has a sense of God's presence led to joy in your experience?

———————————————————————————————

11. As you think about the actions of seeking, remembering and clinging to God, which of these most closely describes what would be most helpful to you at this time? Explain.

Take some time to express your longing for God directly to God.

Now or Later
Based on this study, make a list of specific actions you can take when you are feeling separated from God.

3

A Prayer of Trust

Psalm 62

Humans come into the world as vulnerable creatures, completely dependent on their parents for their survival. For people to develop a healthy capacity to trust, they need to experience an emotional attachment to a nurturing parent. If children are not greeted with nurturing, empathic responses to their physical, emotional and social needs, or if the relationship with the parent is disrupted, the attachment will be threatened and the capacity to trust will be damaged. Later in life it may be more difficult for them to trust God.

The good news is that God can heal our wounds. He can rebuild our capacity to trust.

GROUP DISCUSSION. We all have insecurities in our relationship with God, but we rarely talk about these feelings. Take three to four minutes to write something about your fears and insecurities in relationship to God's trustworthiness. Share what you wrote as you feel comfortable.

PERSONAL REFLECTION. What makes a person trustworthy?

This psalm invites us to risk trusting. It calls us to commit ourselves to God's care. *Read Psalm 62.*

1. How does the writer contrast God and humanity?

2. The psalmist talks about resting in God. What pictures come to your mind with these words?

3. How is resting in God a picture of trust?

4. In verse 8 the psalmist draws a parallel between trusting in God and pouring out one's heart to God. How are these related?

5. Verse 10 warns against trusting in material wealth. How would you paraphrase what is being said here?

6. Why is this such a strong temptation?

7. Where else might you be tempted to place your trust, other than in God?

8. The last two verses depict God as strong and as loving. What images of a strong and loving God are presented in the psalm?

9. What images might you use?

10. How does seeing God as strong help you to trust him?

11. How does seeing God as loving help you to trust him?

Spend some time thanking God for his strength and love and trustworthiness.

Now or Later

Write a psalm (or personal prayer) expressing your current feelings about trusting God. Include any fears, hesitations, longings, hope or gratitude you may have.

4

A Prayer of Distress

Our need for God's presence and care in our lives is a daily reality. We do not always experience this reality, however. As C. S. Lewis wrote in *A Grief Observed*, sometimes "life is so good," we may be "tempted to forget our need of him."* But there are times in our lives when we are acutely aware of our need of God, In times of distress, when we are threatened with loss or harm or even with death, we remember our need of God and we turn to him with great urgency.

Some people feel that they cannot bring their troubles to God. I have often heard people say, "I can't turn to God when I am in distress if I haven't been talking with him all along." And I have heard other people say, "I can't bother God with this, there are many people hurting more than I am." But God invites talking with him when we are in distress. Repeatedly in Scripture God says to us, "Call on me in the day of trouble and I will answer you."

GROUP DISCUSSION. Which of the pictures of God described above do you relate to and why?

PERSONAL REFLECTION. In times of distress do you generally seek out other people or do you withdraw? Explain what you do, and discuss why you might choose these particular behaviors.

This psalm invites us to call on God. The title and the introduction to this psalm suggest that it was written by David when he fled into a cave to hide from King Saul who wanted to kill him. *Read Psalm 57.*

1. Describe the picture of God's comfort David paints in verse 1.

2. What images come to your mind when you think of the experience of being comforted?

3. In his time of distress David cries out to God (v. 2). What does it mean to "cry out" to God?

4. What metaphors does David use in verse 4 to describe the danger he finds himself in?

5. What feelings do these images evoke?

6. How does God intervene for David in his time of distress (vv. 2-3, 6)?

7. David responds to God's care in verse 7 by saying that his heart is steadfast. What is the significance of this response?

8. David also responds with praise to God. Paraphrase the words of praise David offers to God (vv. 5, 9-11).

9. First Samuel 24 tells the story behind this psalm. Read 24:1-7 and 16-20. How did God take care of David in this time of great distress?

10. Hopefully, most of our times of distress will not be as dramatic as this story from David's life. However, any time of distress is a time when our awareness of our need of God may be heightened. Think of a time when you were in distress. Were you able to cry out to God for help at that time? Why or why not?

11. What was your experience of God like during that time?

12. How might this psalm encourage you in times of distress?

Spend some time asking for God's help with the distress you are experiencing in your life today.

Now or Later

Take some time to write about a time when God intervened for you when you were in distress. Write a prayer or a poem thanking God for his help in your time of distress.

*C. S. Lewis, *A Grief Observed* (New York: Bantam, 1976).

5

A Prayer of Gratitude

Because I have difficulty receiving gifts or compliments from others, I have had to remind myself to look people in the eyes when they offer me a gift or a compliment and say thank you.

When we are unable to receive the good things that others offer us, we cheat ourselves, and we cheat them. When we are able to say thank you for gifts given, we are able to take the gift in, enjoy it and engage in a personal, intimate way with the giver of the gift. In the same way, when we express gratitude to God for the gifts he gives us, we enter into a cycle of joyful relating with him. We take in his love, feel a deeper connection with him and experience joy.

GROUP DISCUSSION. Put your names in a hat. Each group member should then draw a name from the hat (make sure no one draws their own name). Take a few minutes to write a note of specific gratitude for the person whose name you drew. Read your notes (either in the whole group, or one on one).

PERSONAL REFLECTION. What is it like for you to receive a gift or a compliment? What is it like for you to offer a gift or compliment to someone else?

The psalmist expresses gratitude to God for a variety of good gifts. *Read Psalm 65.*

1. List four categories of gifts this psalm expresses gratitude for.

2. God's great power is acknowledged in this psalm. How is God's power a gift to us?

3. In verse 5 God is called "our Savior, the hope of all the ends of the earth and of the farthest seas." In what ways is God the hope of all the earth and seas?

4. In what ways is God the source of your hope?

5. The psalmist mentions several of God's awesome deeds in verses 6 and 7. What other awesome deeds might you add to the list?

6. Verse 8 offers a picture of the fears and joys common to all people of the earth. How do God's wonders cause us to experience fear?

7. How do God's wonders call forth songs of joy?

8. Verses 9-13 describe the specific ways in which God tenderly loves and cares for the earth. What thoughts and feelings does this description evoke?

9. What implications does God's care for the earth have for the ways in which we treat the earth?

10. What personal value does expressing gratitude to God have for you?

---

11. What are you grateful for today?

Spend some time expressing your gratitude to God.

Now or Later
Write a psalm of gratitude or a thank-you letter to God expressing your feelings.

6

A Prayer of Grief

Psalm 102

Grief still feels like fear. Perhaps, more strictly, like suspense. Or like waiting; just hanging around waiting for something to happen. It gives life a permanently provisional feeling. . . . The act of living is different all through. Her absence is like the sky, spread over everything.*

Grief is an experience of deep sorrow over a significant loss. Whether the loss we have suffered is the loss of a loved one, a job, our health or our home, the physical, emotional and spiritual suffering is intense. Grieving is an important spiritual and emotional process that allows us to feel the impact of the loss on our lives so that we can slowly take in the reality of our loss and make painful, necessary adaptations. As a part of this process, we need to find people to express our feelings to. And we need to express our feelings over our loss to God.

GROUP DISCUSSION. List on a piece of paper all the losses, big and small, you have experienced in the past few years. Share as much as you want to with the group.

PERSONAL REFLECTION. How would you describe the experience of grief as you have experienced it physically, emotionally and spiritually?

This psalm speaks our anguish to God in times of grief. *Read Psalm 102.*

1. What emotional response do you have toward the psalmist as you read this psalm?

2. How does this psalm contrast the fleeting nature of human life and God's eternal existence?

3. What is the psalmist saying with this contrast?

4. In verses 1-2 the psalmist pleads for God to hear him. Why is this need so urgent in times of grief and distress (vv. 1-2)?

5. How does the psalmist describe his current physical and emotional state (vv. 2-11)?

6. What is it about grief that creates this kind of experience?

7. How do the writer's descriptions of suffering compare with your experiences of grief?

8. Focus on one of the powerful images the writer uses in verses 3-11 to express his suffering. What meaning does the image convey?

9. The psalmist seems to be blaming God and pleading with God at the same time. What does he blame God for (vv. 8, 10, 23)?

10. What does he plead for (vv. 1-2, 24)?

11. The writer seems to have mixed feelings about God. What positive perspectives does he express about God (vv. 12-22, 25-28)?

12. Mixed feelings about God are common in times of suffering and grief. What about times of grief might create these mixed feelings?

13. How could this psalm help you in times of grief?

Spend some time expressing to God whatever grief you may be experiencing for yourself or others.

Now or Later

Write about the mixed feelings you have experienced toward God in times of grief. Spend some time reflecting on the helpfulness of being able to express all of your thoughts and feelings to God.

*C. S. Lewis, *A Grief Observed* (New York: Bantam, 1976), pp. 39, 13.

7

A Prayer When God Is Silent

Psalm 44

Is not God silent about Stalingrad? What do we hear above and under its ruins? Do we not hear the roar of artillery, the tumult of the world and the cries of the dying? But where is the voice of God? When we think of God, is it not suddenly so quiet, so terribly quiet, in the witch's kitchen of this hell, that one can hear a pin drop even though grenades are bursting around us? There is neither voice nor answer.*

We have not all lived through the atrocities of war. But we all are vulnerable to loss and trauma. The silence of God is perhaps one of life's most frightening experiences. What do we do? How do we proceed when God is silent? Do we withdraw in fear? Do we give up all hope? That is certainly our temptation.

GROUP DISCUSSION. Think of a time when a friend did not respond to letters or phone messages for a long time. What was your reaction to his or her silence?

PERSONAL REFLECTION. Think of a time when you asked for God's help and did not sense any help or response from God.

Write two or three words on paper that describe some of what you thought or felt at that time.

This psalm shows the way for us to pursue God even when he is silent. *Read Psalm 44.*

1. What anguish do you hear in this psalm?

2. How does the writer contrast God in the past (vv. 1-8) with God in the present (vv. 9-16)?

3. What strikes you as you read the writer's description of God's care?

4. What strikes you as you read the writer's description of God's silence?

5. The psalmist argues with God that the situation he and his people find themselves in is not fair. How does he express this (vv. 17-22)?

6. What is the significance of this plea for fairness and justice?

7. The psalmist summarizes his accusations against God in verses 23 and 24. What does he accuse God of?

8. What would it be like for you to talk to God in this way?

9. In the final phrase of the psalm, the writer appeals to God's unfailing love. This is a dramatic contrast to the accusations he has just made. How can these be reconciled?

10. Think of a time when it seemed God was silent. How did your experience at that time compare with the experiences described in this psalm?

11. Think of a time when you experienced God's unfailing love. How would you describe that experience?

12. What encouragement does this psalm offer you for times when God seems silent?

13. What might help you hang on to your faith when God seems silent?

Spend some time talking to God about your need to know his presence with you in difficult times.

Now or Later

Often it is helpful in difficult times to remember times when we could see God's love and care for us. Consider starting a journal devoted to such moments: write about several events from the past when you were aware of God's care for you, and keep the journal handy to continue adding to it.

---

*Helmut Thielicke, *The Silence of God* (Grand Rapids, Mich.: Eerdmans, 1962).

8

A Prayer for Hope

Psalm 130

During a time of difficult waiting I expressed the contrast between waiting with hope and waiting without hope:

When waiting is expectant,
I move through the light and shadows
of life's in-between times content.
Able to see the apricot tree laced with white explosions
while it is yet dead wood.
Able to hear in the silence the music of your voice,
greeting me with grace.
But when waiting is threatened,
I bear in raging anguish the nightmare possibility
of no return of spring or you.
Waiting stretches me across a torture rack of longing.
Afraid to hope or want or breathe again.
Blind, deaf, cold with fright
I wait.

Hope is necessary. It gives us the strength to keep going through the tough times. It gives life joy and meaning in the good times. But sometimes it's hard to hold on to.

GROUP DISCUSSION. Take ten minutes to work in pairs, cutting pictures from magazines to make small collages (one collage per pair). Half of the pairs should make collages of images of hope, including both situations that strengthen our hope and images of hopefulness. The other half of the pairs should make collages of images of hopelessness, including situations that create hopelessness and images of hopelessness. Take time to discuss each collage.

PERSONAL REFLECTION. How would you personally describe the experience of hope? How would you personally describe the experience of hopelessness?

When hope has been repeatedly disappointed, it slips away. This psalm offers a picture of this struggle. The writer is without much hope. Yet, he puts himself in a place of allowing for the possibility of hope. As we pray with him, we too can begin to wait with growing expectation. *Read Psalm 130.*

1. The psalm begins with a cry to the Lord from "out of the depths" (v. 1). What pictures come to mind as you read this phrase?

2. What emotions is the writer expressing in this phrase?

3. The psalmist's distress seems to be related to a struggle with guilt (v. 3). How can guilt lead to hopelessness?

4. Verses 3 and 4 tell us that God forgives. How does the promise of forgiveness contribute to hope?

5. Verse 5 says, "I wait . . . my soul waits." What is the relationship between waiting and hope?

6. The psalmist then uses the metaphor of watchmen (v. 6) to describe the experience of hope. What does he convey with this image?

7. The psalmist struggles between hopelessness and hope. Why is it sometimes a struggle to hope?

8. What area of life is difficult for you to be hopeful about?

9. What reasons does the psalmist give for hoping in the Lord (vv. 7-8)?

10. What reasons do you have for hoping in the Lord?

11. How have you grown spiritually as you have struggled to wait with hope for the Lord?

12. How might this psalm help you to hope in the Lord?

Spend some time acknowledging to God the ways in which you struggle to hold on to hope.

Now or Later

Spend some time reflecting on verses 7 and 8. Write about your thoughts and feelings during this time of reflection.

9

A Prayer of Joy

Psalm 66

Life was not intended by God to be a joyless ordeal. As much as it might surprise some of us, it is actually God's desire for us to experience joy. Joy is an act of relating to God with vulnerable, unselfconscious gratitude for the good gifts he gives. Joy comes when we experience and acknowledge God's love and care for us, when we allow ourselves to express our gratitude for his love with emotional and physical energy. Joy is the celebration of God's love.

GROUP DISCUSSION. Plan ahead to have a time of celebration. Bring noisemakers, streamers, party hats and food. Bring words of gratitude to God for what you have experienced in these weeks of studying Psalms. Enjoy a time of celebration together.

PERSONAL REFLECTION. Think of a time when you experienced joy. What evoked this feeling in you? How would you describe the experience of joy?

This psalm invites us to experience joy. *Read Psalm 66.*

1. The writer calls us to action (vv. 1, 2, 3, 5, 8 and 16). What does he call us to do?

2. How are each of these behaviors related to the experience or the expression of joy?

3. What does the section in the middle of this psalm (vv. 8-12) tell us about the cause for this particular expression of joy?

4. How might this kind of experience lead to joy?

5. Verses 13-15 talk about offering animal sacrifices as an expression of joy and worship. A person's livestock was the equivalent of our personal bank accounts. How can giving materially be an expression of gratitude and joy?

6. Verses 16-20 are a more personal account of what the Lord has done. What does the writer say the Lord has done for him?

7. How might this kind of experience lead to joy?

8. In addition to the actions listed in question 2, what ways of expressing joy to God are described in this psalm?

9. What other ways of expressing joy to God would you add?

10. In what ways are joy, praise and worship related?

11. It is important to realize that this psalm is not about pretending to be joyful when it is more honest or appropriate to be grieving or angry. What dangers are there in pretending to be joyful when we are not?

12. Why is it important to allow ourselves to experience and express joy?

13. What joy would you like to express to God?

Take some time to express your joy to God in a time of prayer.

Now or Later
Make a list of all the gifts God has given you that contribute to your joy.

Leader's Notes

Leading a Bible discussion can be an enjoyable and rewarding experience. But it can also be *scary*—especially if you've never done it before. If this is your feeling, you're in good company. When God asked Moses to lead the Israelites out of Egypt, he replied, "O Lord, please send someone else to do it!" (Ex 4:13). It was the same with Solomon, Jeremiah and Timothy, but God helped these people in spite of their weaknesses, and he will help you as well.

You don't need to be an expert on the Bible or a trained teacher to lead a Bible discussion. The idea behind these inductive studies is that the leader guides group members to discover for themselves what the Bible has to say. This method of learning will allow group members to remember much more of what is said than a lecture would.

These studies are designed to be led easily. As a matter of fact, the flow of questions through the passage from observation to interpretation to application is so natural that you may feel that the studies lead themselves. This study guide is also flexible. You can use it with a variety of groups—student, professional, neighborhood or church groups. Each study takes forty-five to sixty minutes in a group setting.

There are some important facts to know about group dynamics and encouraging discussion. The suggestions listed below should enable you to effectively and enjoyably fulfill your role as leader.

Preparing for the Study

1. Ask God to help you understand and apply the passage in your

own life. Unless this happens, you will not be prepared to lead others. Pray too for the various members of the group. Ask God to open your hearts to the message of his Word and motivate you to action.

2. Read the introduction to the entire guide to get an overview of the entire book and the issues which will be explored.

3. As you begin each study, read and reread the assigned Bible passage to familiarize yourself with it.

4. This study guide is based on the New International Version of the Bible. It will help you and the group if you use this translation as the basis for your study and discussion.

5. Carefully work through each question in the study. Spend time in meditation and reflection as you consider how to respond.

6. Write your thoughts and responses in the space provided in the study guide. This will help you to express your understanding of the passage clearly.

7. It might help to have a Bible dictionary handy. Use it to look up any unfamiliar words, names or places. (For additional help on how to study a passage, see chapter five of *How to Lead a LifeBuilder Study*, IVP, 2018.)

8. Consider how you can apply the Scripture to your life. Remember that the group will follow your lead in responding to the studies. They will not go any deeper than you do.

9. Once you have finished your own study of the passage, familiarize yourself with the leader's notes for the study you are leading. These are designed to help you in several ways. First, they tell you the purpose the study guide author had in mind when writing the study. Take time to think through how the study questions work together to accomplish that purpose. Second, the notes provide you with additional background information or suggestions on group dynamics for various questions. This information can be useful when people have difficulty understanding or answering a question. Third, the leader's notes can alert you to potential problems you may encounter during the study.

10. If you wish to remind yourself of anything mentioned in the leader's notes, make a note to yourself below that question in the study.

Leading the Study

1. Begin the study on time. Open with prayer, asking God to help the group to understand and apply the passage.

2. Be sure that everyone in your group has a study guide. Encourage the group to prepare beforehand for each discussion by reading the introduction to the guide and by working through the questions in the study.

3. At the beginning of your first time together, explain that these studies are meant to be discussions, not lectures. Encourage the members of the group to participate. However, do not put pressure on those who may be hesitant to speak during the first few sessions. You may want to suggest the following guidelines to your group.

☐ Stick to the topic being discussed.

☐ Your responses should be based on the verses which are the focus of the discussion and not on outside authorities such as commentaries or speakers.

☐ These studies focus on a particular passage of Scripture. Only rarely should you refer to other portions of the Bible. This allows for everyone to participate in in-depth study on equal ground.

☐ Anything said in the group is considered confidential and will not be discussed outside the group unless specific permission is given to do so.

☐ We will listen attentively to each other and provide time for each person present to talk.

☐ We will pray for each other.

4. Have a group member read the introduction at the beginning of the discussion.

5. Every session begins with a group discussion question. The question or activity is meant to be used before the passage is read. The question introduces the theme of the study and encourages group members to begin to open up. Encourage as many members as possible to participate, and be ready to get the discussion going with your own response.

This section is designed to reveal where our thoughts or feelings need to be transformed by Scripture. That is why it is especially important not to read the passage before the discussion question is asked. The passage will tend to color the honest reactions people would otherwise give because they are, of course, supposed to think the way the Bible does.

You may want to supplement the group discussion question with an icebreaker to help people to get comfortable. See the community section of the *Small Group Starter Kit* (IVP, 1995) for more ideas.

You also might want to use the personal reflection question with your group. Either allow a time of silence for people to respond individually or discuss it together.

6. Have a group member (or members if the passage is long) read aloud the passage to be studied. Then give people several minutes to read the passage again silently so that they can take it all in.

7. Question 1 will generally be an overview question designed to briefly survey the passage. Encourage the group to look at the whole passage, but try to avoid getting sidetracked by questions or issues that will be addressed later in the study.

8. As you ask the questions, keep in mind that they are designed to be used just as they are written. You may simply read them aloud. Or you may prefer to express them in your own words.

There may be times when it is appropriate to deviate from the study guide. For example, a question may have already been answered. If so, move on to the next question. Or someone may raise an important question not covered in the guide. Take time to discuss it, but try to keep the group from going off on tangents.

9. Avoid answering your own questions. If necessary, repeat or rephrase them until they are clearly understood. Or point out something you read in the leader's notes to clarify the context or meaning. An eager group quickly becomes passive and silent if they think the leader will do most of the talking.

10. Don't be afraid of silence. People may need time to think about the question before formulating their answers.

11. Don't be content with just one answer. Ask, "What do the rest of you think?" or "Anything else?" until several people have given answers to the question.

12. Acknowledge all contributions. Try to be affirming whenever possible. Never reject an answer. If it is clearly off-base, ask, "Which verse led you to that conclusion?" or again, "What do the rest of you think?"

13. Don't expect every answer to be addressed to you, even though this will probably happen at first. As group members become more at ease, they will begin to truly interact with each other. This is one sign of healthy discussion.

14. Don't be afraid of controversy. It can be very stimulating. If you don't resolve an issue completely, don't be frustrated. Move on and keep it in mind for later. A subsequent study may solve the problem.

15. Periodically summarize what the group has said about the passage. This helps to draw together the various ideas mentioned and gives continuity to the study. But don't preach.

16. At the end of the Bible discussion you may want to allow group members a time of quiet to work on an idea under "Now or Later." Then discuss what you experienced. Or you may want to encourage group members to work on these ideas between meetings. Give an opportunity during the session for people to talk about what they are learning.

17. Conclude your time together with conversational prayer, adapting the prayer suggestion at the end of the study to your group. Ask for God's help in following through on the commitments you've made.

18. End on time.

Many more suggestions and helps are found in *How to Lead a LifeBuilder Study*.

Components of Small Groups

A healthy small group should do more than study the Bible. There are four components to consider as you structure your time together.

Nurture. Small groups help us to grow in our knowledge and love of God. Bible study is the key to making this happen and is the foundation of your small group.

Community. Small groups are a great place to develop deep friendships with other Christians. Allow time for informal interaction before and after each study. Plan activities and games that will help you get to know each other. Spend time having fun together—going on a picnic or cooking dinner together.

Worship and prayer. Your study will be enhanced by spending time praising God together in prayer or song. Pray for each other's needs—and keep track of how God is answering prayer in your group. Ask God to help you to apply what you are learning in your study.

Outreach. Reaching out to others can be a practical way of applying what you are learning, and it will keep your group from becoming self-focused. Host a series of evangelistic discussions for your friends or neighbors. Clean up the yard of an elderly friend. Serve at a soup kitchen together, or spend a day working in the community.

Many more suggestions and helps in each of these areas are found in the *Small Group Starter Kit.* You will also find information on building a small group. Reading through the starter kit will be worth your time.

General Note

The psalms are deeply emotive prayers, written in the intense language of poetry. To engage with the psalms is to engage strong feelings. Members of the group will have different responses to talking together about feelings. Talking and listening to feelings may come easily for some. For others, talking or listening to emotional pain may feel uncomfortable.

Acknowledge both that the psalms are full of strong feelings and that there is bound to be some discomfort in talking together about feelings. The group might want to take time to discuss what they anticipate, expect, fear and need in regard to this issue. Make it clear that people always have a choice about what they share, and that no one is required to share when it is uncomfortable to do so. On the other hand, groups such as this provide the opportunity for stretching and growing, so some risk-taking and "moving out of one's comfort zone" can be a good thing.

The group needs to agree on two commitments. First, whatever is shared in the group will be treated as confidential and will not be shared outside the group without specific permission from the person. And second, they will listen to each other with respect—

being cautious about giving advice and solutions, responding to the person who shared with simple statements of gratitude for their sharing.

A very helpful way to interact with the psalms is to write a responsive psalm of one's own, expressing similar feelings or concerns as those expressed in that particular psalm. This is something your group might want to do with each psalm. If so, it is important to know that this is not meant to be a creative-writing exercise but a free-writing exercise. It is an opportunity to write out a prayer in whatever form it takes. Encourage people not to edit, but to write as spontaneously as they can. Invite those who want to read their psalms out loud as a prayer.

Study 1. A Prayer of Dependence. Psalm 86.
Purpose: To acknowledge our dependency on God.
Question 2. Note the writer's direct, frank, unselfconscious expression of need. The psalmist evidences a sense of childlike dependence on God's love and goodness.
Question 4. In describing himself as "poor and needy," the psalmist is honestly acknowledging his need and appealing to God for help. He is needy, and since God made him and his needs, he brings himself and his needs to God. George MacDonald offered a perspective on this when he wrote:

> It is God to whom every hunger, every aspiration, every desire, every longing of our nature is to be referred. He made them all—made us the creatures of a thousand necessities—and have we no claim on him? . . . The child has and must have, a claim on the Father, a claim which it is the joy of the Father's heart to acknowledge. A created need is a created claim. God is the origin of both need and supply, the Father of our necessities, the abundant giver of the good things. Gloriously he meets the claims of his child! (*Discovering the Character of God*, compiled by Michael R. Phillips [Minneapolis: Bethany House, 1989], pp. 206-7)

Question 5. The reactions of the group to describing themselves as "poor and needy" will, of course, be varied. But it is common for us to be very uncomfortable with such a description. We want to be self-reliant and independent. We are not. It is a myth that protects us from the painful reality that we are vulnerable.

Question 6. The psalmist needs help because "the arrogant are attacking" him, "a band of ruthless men" are seeking his life (v. 14). The psalmist is facing a situation that is too big for him. He is overwhelmed.

It might be useful to point out that most people do not have someone stalking them to kill them. But there will be times when our lives or the life of someone close to us may be threatened with illness. There may be times when we feel threatened in other ways (financially, for example) that are overwhelming to us. We all experience many days that would qualify as "days of trouble" (v. 7). We all need God's help in ways similar to what the psalmist experienced. We all have troubles that are too big for us to handle alone.

Question 9. The group may have difficulty identifying evidence of dependence on God. The psalmist identifies his neediness and contrasts it with God's love and power. He makes many direct requests and appeals that come out of his needs. He clearly knows he cannot take care of himself. He knows he needs God.

Question 10. One reason we may have a need to see ourselves as self-sufficient is that many of us experienced shaming for our needs in our most dependent years. Because parents are less than perfect, and sometimes significantly less than what we needed, the experience of being actively cared for by someone who is loving and powerful may feel unfamiliar to us. To begin to see God in this way can help us give up our defense of self-sufficiency and begin to let ourselves depend on God more fully.

Question 11. The psalmist models a level of honest humility and dependency on God that our society tends to scorn. His example can give us permission to acknowledge the reality of our need of God, and his expression can help us find ways of expressing those needs specifically.

Study 2. A Prayer of Longing for God. Psalm 63.

Purpose: To express our longing for God in times when we feel separated from him.

Question 2. This metaphor might be seen in several ways. It is a metaphor of dying. It is a metaphor of intense suffering and longing. And it is a metaphor of a person with a single-minded focus—there is only one thing in all the world that a thirsty person in a desert wants. We need God in the same way that we need water. They are basic to life. When we see no sign of God anywhere, we experience deep suffering and intense longing, and we might fear that we will die.

Question 3. The psalmist felt closest to God when he was in the sanctuary—in the place of worship, with a community of believers. You might want to encourage the group to discuss the role of the community of believers in their experience of closeness to God. Some may have had negative experiences with churches. Some may relate very much to what the psalmist is expressing.

Question 6. Help the group discuss the perspectives and the behaviors involved in seeking God. Perspectives might include a sense of awareness, of being on the lookout for, of being open to, of being motivated to find. Behaviors might include studying Scripture, praying and being with other believers.

Question 9. In Deuteronomy 30:20 we are told to "love the LORD your God, listen to his voice, and hold fast to him." Clinging—or holding fast—to God brings to mind a young child hanging on for dear life to a loving parent. This might be a comforting image for some. For others it might be difficult. Give the group permission to discuss their honest reactions.

Now or Later. These lists can be done individually and then discussed by the group, or the group can make a list together.

Study 3. A Prayer of Trust. Psalm 62.

Purpose: To learn to rest more fully in God's love.

Question 1. God is described as a rock, a refuge, a fortress, a place of rest and safety that is reliable, permanent, constant. God is also described as strong and loving. Humanity, by contrast, is described as opportunistic (they fully intend to topple this tottering wall, v. 3), deceitful (blessing with the mouth while cursing with the heart, v. 4) and "only a breath" (v. 9).

Question 3. Resting and trust both have to do with relaxing, letting go of anxiety, leaning into, feeling held and feeling secure enough to let down our guard and be vulnerable.

Question 4. You might help the group talk about what is involved when we pour out our heart to someone. It involves intimate disclosure of our deepest needs and feelings. It is a vulnerable act that is possible only when we have some sense that the other person will not judge us or reject us or mock us. It is based in trust that the other person will listen, care, understand, empathize and respond to us.

Question 8. When the images of *mighty rock, refuge* and *fortress* are understood to be set in the open desert, where the sun was scorching, the wind could be merciless and one could be an easy prey to enemies, these images take on new depth. In these images God is seen as reliable, kind, protective, concerned. He is always there to run to, to hold us, protect us, comfort us and care for us. He is strong. He is loving. More specifically, he is strong and loving on our behalf.

Question 9. Encourage the group to put some effort into coming up with images of God as strong and loving. The images used in the psalms came out of common material realities of the day; we do not see fortresses on our way to work. Images are powerful when they are connected to our everyday experiences. Encourage the group to discuss the significance of the images they do come up with. You might ask: "What does the image mean to you?" or "What would it be like to see God in this way?"

Now or Later. Information on writing a responsive psalm is at the beginning of this section under "general note."

Study 4. A Prayer of Distress. Psalm 57.
Purpose: To learn to call on God in times of distress.

Group Discussion. If it is comfortable for your group, you could open in the following way: invite members of the group to share any distress they are experiencing at the present time. Pray for each other.

Question 1. Encourage the group to reflect on the image of taking refuge in the shadow of God's wings. This can be seen as a chick hiding under his mother's wing. It is a picture of being incredibly close, of being protected, of being intimately loved. It is also a picture of the hen putting herself between the chick and his aggressor, protecting him with her life.

Question 3. The group might need help to see that "crying out" is an instinctive, heartfelt, urgent, desperate call for help. When we "cry out," there is no time for face-saving measures or for pretense. When we "cry out," we reveal ourselves; we are real. This is how the psalms help us to relate to God.

> This is the language of prayer: men and women calling out their trouble—pain, guilt, doubt, despair—to God. Their lives are threatened. If they don't get help they will be dead, or diminished to some critical degree. The language of prayer is forged in the crucible of trouble. When we can't help ourselves and call for help, when we don't like where we are and want out, when we don't like who we are and want a change, we use primal language, and this language becomes the root language of prayer. . . . We must let the Psalms train us in prayer language—the language of intimacy, of relationship, of "I and Thou," of personal love. (Eugene Peterson, *Answering God* [San Francisco: Harper & Row, 1989], pp. 35, 40)

Question 7. To be steadfast is to be deeply committed to another person. Help the group discuss both the difficulty and the value of staying committed to God in times of distress.

Question 9. Saul, who was a madman by this time, took three thousand of his finest fighting men with him to hunt down David and his men. It must have seemed an impossible situation. But God protected David in an unexpected way.

It would be helpful to point out that there is a comic nature to the story of Saul relieving himself in the dark cave where David hid. God took the madman Saul away from his three thousand men and put him in a vulnerable situation with David. This unexpected, creative, surprising twist to the story should not be missed.

Question 10. Encourage the group to discuss the permission that this psalm, and others, gives for relating to God out of our need. The psalms can free us. They can help us get past our shame and fear. They can help us be childlike with God.

Study 5. A Prayer of Gratitude. Psalm 65.

Purpose: To experience the joy of saying "thank you" to God.

Question 1. The psalmist expresses gratitude for forgiveness (v. 3), relationship (vv. 4-5), creation (vv. 6-8) and sustaining, loving care (vv. 9-13).

Question 2. God is powerful. This can be either good news or bad news. Help the group to discuss the significance of the fact that God uses his power to help us, not as a weapon to harm us. In this psalm we reflect on how God uses his power to protect, provide, create and save.

Question 3. You might help the group identify God as the "hope of the earth and seas" by leading a brief discussion about the many ways God sustains the earth and all living things. As Creator, he is highly involved in an ongoing way with his creation. More specifically for us as humans, he is our hope as Creator, Sustainer and Savior.

Question 5. Encourage all kinds of responses from the group. There are many awesome deeds that God does, some global, some very personal.

Question 6. Help the group discuss the meaning of the fear of God that we experience when we see his wonders. It is a fear that is based in the reality that God is all-powerful, that he is the Creator and we are creatures, that he is infinite and we are finite. It is a fear out of respect and appropriate humility. The contrasting joy in response to these same wonders is intriguing. We experience joy because we see that God uses his power to provide us with gifts of beauty and life.

Question 9. This text describes God's tender love for all he has made and compels us to share his perspective. God has given us the gift of his creation. One way to express gratitude for a gift is to cherish it and take good care of it.

Study 6. A Prayer of Grief. Psalm 102.

Purpose: To learn to pray in times of grief.

Question 2. It is important to realize that the psalmist did not have a sense of life after death.

It seems quite clear that in most parts of the Old Testament there is little or no belief in a future life; certainly no belief that is of any religious importance. The word translated "Sheol" in our version of the psalms means simply "the land of the dead," the state of all the dead, good and bad alike, Sheol. (C. S. Lewis, *Reflections on the Psalms* [New York: Harcourt, Brace & World, 1958], p. 36)

As a result, the psalmist is saying to God, "It really isn't fair that you should cut me off in midlife, when my life as a human is so short and your life is eternal. It isn't fair, and what good will it do anybody?"

Question 4. Help the group discuss the reality that we can feel separated from God in times of loss or distress, because it can feel as if God has forgotten us or turned away from us when bad things happen. This sense of separation from God adds a spiritual crisis on top of the original crisis of the loss. We very much need to feel God's presence when we are faced with loss, yet we may feel his absence instead. It is out of this struggle that the psalmist speaks with such urgency to God.

Question 6. Grief is a powerful physical, emotional and spiritual experience. Sometimes when we lose someone or something close to us we say we feel as if "we have lost a part of ourselves." We become deeply attached to people, places and dreams. The loss of any of these requires an enormous adaptation on our part—one that we would rather avoid.

Years ago I spoke to a twenty-year-old woman whose father had died when she was eight. She had never grieved losing him. She had spent the twelve years after his death imagining that he would come back and that life would be like it was before he left. This fantasy had left her out of touch with reality, unable to cope or to form new relationships. But to face the reality of his death was to feel the full impact of the loss. She needed, as we all do, support from others to do the hard work of grieving. This hard work ("grief work") requires that we talk at length about the person or place or object or dream that we have lost, feel the sadness and anger and fear the loss creates, and slowly accept the reality.

Question 7. Give the group permission to share their honest reactions to the writer's suffering. They may feel repulsion or identification; they may feel like they don't want to hear about it, or they may feel empathy. Whatever each person might feel at the time, there is a reason for their reaction. If members seem to feel comfortable, you might ask them what makes them react the way they do.

Question 11. This question is related to the discussion in study 2 on longing for God. Because the experience of loss and grief can leave us feeling separated from God, as if he has left us, we may react with the mixture of feelings that small children have when separated from their parents. We may feel anger, fear and a deep yearning to reunite with God.

Question 13. If it feels comfortable and if time allows, you may want to conclude with the following question: "What grief are you aware of (over a loss you have suffered—recent or long past) that you need to express to God?" Use this as a basis for praying for one another.

Study 7. A Prayer When God Is Silent. Psalm 44.
Purpose: To discover that we need to pray, even when God is silent.

Question 3. You might want to focus especially on verse 3, which is highly personal in its expression of the experience of God's love.

Question 4. Discuss the uncomfortable fact that the way the psalmist describes God's silence is that he sees God as cruel, as actively punishing them by his lack of responsiveness. This is not a doctrinal statement asserting that God is cruel. It is a statement from the gut about how it feels when God is not responsive to us, when he does not save or protect us.

Question 9. The group may need help to see that the whole psalm is actually an appeal to God's love. It is because of God's love that God will not want his people to experience his silence as harshness. It is because of his love that he will eventually respond to their need.

Question 13. It is important for the group to realize that when it seems that God is silent, they are not alone with this experience. Many people struggle with this from time to time, including many of God's most faithful. If we are able to talk about our experience with other believers and ask for their support, understanding and prayers, we will not be so alone in these times. Be sure to pray for each other, and reach out to any in the group who may be feeling discouraged in some way.

Study 8. A Prayer for Hope. Psalm 130.

Purpose: To nurture hope.

Questions 3-4. The group will undoubtedly see that guilt separates us from God and that forgiveness restores our relationship with him. But the further question here is, "Why is our hope so tied to our relationship with God?" The answer has to do with the nature of hope. Hope is not necessarily believing that everything will be fine. Hope is believing that God will be with us no matter what happens.

Question 5. It is important to note that waiting for God and waiting for hope are seen as one and the same, because our hope is in God.

> We need to remind ourselves daily that we do not serve the god-of-relentless-cheerfulness, or the god-of-naiveté, or the god-of-blind-optimism. We serve the God of hope. . . . We can come to him with our fear, doubt and despair and God will give good gifts to us. When all other reasons for hope fail us, we can return to the God of hope because he is greater than our disappointment, greater than our failure, greater than the problems and conflicts in our hearts and our homes and our communities and our world. (Dale and Juanita Ryan, *Rooted in God's Love* [Downers Grove, Ill.: InterVarsity Press, 1992], pp. 241-42)

Question 7. There are many reasons that we struggle to hope. Sometimes it seems that there is no reason to hope, that all evidence points to the contrary. Sometimes it seems like too much of a risk to hope because we do not feel we can live through another disappointment.

Study 9. A Prayer of Joy. Psalm 66.

Purpose: To teach us how to express joy.

Question 4. The joy in this section is related to the experience of being delivered from danger. Encourage the group to discuss how the experience of coming through a difficult time can lead to joy.

Question 5. Giving materially puts many things into perspective. It is a tangible way of expressing the truth that all we have comes from God and belongs to God. It is a tangible way of saying thank you. And expressing gratitude is very closely related to expressing joy.

Question 7. Here joy is related to the experience of being personally loved. You might help the group discuss the relationship between experiencing God's love in personal ways and experiencing joy.

Question 12. Encourage the group to focus on the expression of joy as an act of intimate relating to God. This is one reason that joy is important. It is also important because we need to allow ourselves to experience the full rainbow of emotions God made us capable of feeling.

Juanita Ryan is a mental health nurse specialist with a private counseling practice in Brea, California. She is also the author of four Women of Character Bible Studies. She and her husband, Dale, authored the Life Recovery Guides and the Letting God Be God Bible Studies. The Ryans have over a half million Bible study guides in print.